THE FRAGRANT ART OF

AROMATHERAPY

*An introduction to aromatherapy
and the use of essential oils*

Linda Doeser

CLB

Designed and produced by

THE BRIDGEWATER BOOK COMPANY LTD

Designed by *Peter Laws/Peter Bridgewater*

Managing Editor (CLB) *Jo Finnis*

Typesetting & page makeup by *Lee Forster*

Watercolour illustrations (pages 15, 17, 21, 23, 30, 32, 37, 40, 44) by *Nicola Gregory*

Cover photograph by *John Glover/Garden Picture Library*

CLB 4747

© 1995 COLOUR LIBRARY BOOKS LTD

Godalming, Surrey, England.

Colour separations by Tien Wah Press, Singapore

Printed in Singapore by Tien Wah Press

ISBN 1-85833-488-8

Contents

Introduction

S MELL is probably the most basic — and most potent — of all human instincts. Our Neolithic ancestors followed their noses to find food, detect enemies and track down a mate. Just a short way into the story of human civilization, culinary and medicinal herbs became a part of daily life, their aromatic qualities soon playing equally important roles for both function and fun.

The ancient Egyptians burned aromatic gums and resins in elaborate religious rituals, while the ancient Romans soon discovered the mood-enhancing joys of sweet smells. In the Middle Ages, as successive plagues swept across Europe and the Middle East, physicians and herbalists once again searched the plant kingdom for cures and preventative measures. Flowers, fruit, leaves, resins, barks and herbs that are still well known today played an essential role in the treatment of illness throughout history — rosemary, sage, peppermint, oranges and cloves, for example.

Across the world, wise men — and women — sought natural cures for weaknesses of both mind and body. Maoris in New Zealand used the plant now called tea-tree for bathing cuts, wounds and burns. Modern science has since revealed it to be a powerful antiseptic. Native Americans treated skin conditions with an infusion of spruce — now analysed as being rich in vitamin C.

The story of aromatherapy as formal science, however, does not begin until 1937. The French chemist René Maurice Gattefossé

From ancient times perfumes have been valued for their spicy fragrances.

was working in the laboratory of a perfumery when he burned his hand. To relieve the pain, he plunged it into the nearest container of cold liquid which, by happy coincidence, was lavender oil. His hand healed astonishingly quickly with little or no scarring. He was so impressed by this that he resolved to investigate the medicinal powers of other essential oils and devoted the remainder of his life to the study of aromathérapie.

Gradually, interest spread across Europe, finally reaching Britain and then extending to the United States. It is no coincidence that this rising interest in aromatherapy has happened at a time when people are becoming more conscious of the dangerous side-effects of the potent drugs of conventional medicine and are simultaneously expressing a desire to take more responsibility for their own health and well-being.

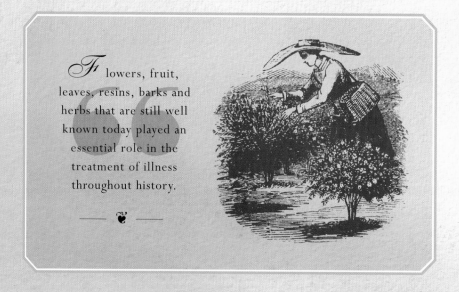

*F*lowers, fruit, leaves, resins, barks and herbs that are still well known today played an essential role in the treatment of illness throughout history.

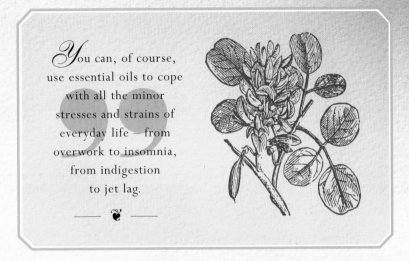

You can, of course, use essential oils to cope with all the minor stresses and strains of everyday life – from overwork to insomnia, from indigestion to jet lag.

Treatment of serious illness is best left to a qualified aromatherapist, who will take a holistic approach to your condition and who will have a thorough knowledge of the physical and psychological effects of the essential oils. If you are seeking treatment for a medical condition, such as arthritis, eczema, psoriasis, high blood pressure or varicose veins, all of which are recorded as responding positively to aromatherapy, consult your regular medical practitioner first.

You can, of course, use essential oils to cope with all the minor stresses and strains of everyday life – from a headache to a hangover, overwork to insomnia, indigestion to jet lag.

In the following pages you will find suggestions for different ways to use essential oils, some hints on massage, a word of warning concerning specific oils and conditions when their use is contra-indicated and an oil-by-oil guide to some of the most popular and useful oils available.

How it works

ONCE upon a time, people relied on their sense of smell for their very survival. These days, we tend to be aware of only those smells which are either quite delightful or completely horrible. However, subconsciously, our brains register thousands of other smells and respond to them. The aroma of freshly baked bread stimulates the appetite and the scent of orange blossom can transport us to a holiday island miles — and years — away. Smell evokes emotions as well as physical responses and memories.

Smell receptors in the nose are exposed directly to the air. With each breath — and we take over 20,000 breaths each day — they take in scents. The brain recognizes and responds to smells faster than it does to any other of our senses.

The brain's response to the stimulation of smell is complex and not yet fully understood. Nevertheless, we all instinctively recognize that smell has an effect on mood and emotions. We use this knowledge every time we give someone a bunch of sweet-smelling flowers, for example. They immediately lighten the mood and spread a feeling of warmth. We do the same thing when we soak in a hot bath scented with perfumed

"We all instinctively recognize that smell has an effect on mood and emotions."

oils to relax and ease the tension at the end of a busy day.

Science has now begun to catch up and serious research into the effects of smell is taking place in Britain, the United States and Japan. Computers have been programmed for biochemical analysis of smells, while others measure and record changes in brainwaves brought about by smell during clinical trials. What science probably cannot demonstrate is the sheer pleasure of using aromatherapy to relieve unpleasant symptoms, relax a tense body and mind and simply to make you feel wonderful.

Essential oils

A<small>T THE</small> heart of aromatherapy are essential oils – 'concentrated smells'. No one is completely sure exactly what they are, although scientists have analysed many of their chemical constituents. They are naturally occurring substances found in tiny sacs in different parts of plants: flowers, leaves, bark, berries, stems and roots. Different parts of the same plant may produce various oils. For example, pettigrain comes from orange leaves, orange oil from the peel of the fruit and neroli from the blossom.

Extracting essential oils is a complicated process and may be very expensive. Many are obtained by distillation. The relevant part of the plant is processed by steam in a vat and the oil is then separated from the cooled, condensed water. Lavender oil is produced this way. Essential oils from very fragile flowers, such as ylang ylang and jasmine, are obtained by solvent extraction because the heat and pressure of distillation would destroy the oil. Oils extracted by this method are called absolutes – rose absolute, for example. Oils from fruit peel are squeezed into special sponges, barks are usually powdered before distillation and gums and resins are dissolved in solvents.

OILS OF SANDALWOOD, ROSEMARY AND MYRRH

Essential oils are extremely volatile, but not at all greasy. They are usually supplied in dark glass bottles and should be stored in the bottles, in a cool place and out of direct sunlight. Do not use plastic containers, as they can be damaged by the oils.

It is important to buy oils from a reputable source as this not only guarantees purity, but quality as well. Rather like wine, essential oils have good and bad years. Look for the words 'pure essential oil' on the label of the bottle, as synthetic oils and diluted mixtures do not have the same potency. Price varies according to the source of the oil. Many very useful oils are fairly inexpensive. Others are a very self-indulgent and luxurious treat. It takes 2,000 kg of rose petals to produce 30 ml of oil and 8,000 kg of jasmine blossom for the same quantity. It is hardly surprising, therefore, that the price is high.

Using essential oils

THERE are numerous ways of using essential oils and benefiting from their powerful effects.

Massage is the technique mainly used by professional aromatherapists and is the best known and most effective way of using the oils. It stimulates the circulation so that the oils are rapidly carried around the body and the warmth generated by rubbing them on the skin tends to make them smell stronger. You can massage yourself very successfully, although some parts of the body, such as the back and shoulders, really cannot be comfortably reached. Massaging someone else provides a special kind of intimacy. Touch is a much underrated form of communication and is a powerful force for cementing loving relationships.

> *Touch is a much underrated form of communication and is a powerful force for cementing loving relationships.*

Essential oils are very potent so they should never be used undiluted. For massage they must be blended with a carrier oil. Almost any vegetable oil is suitable — it does not have to be expensive. Extra virgin cold-pressed oils are best and it is wise to avoid those, such as olive and corn oil, with a strong smell themselves. Luxurious carrier oils are peach nut, apricot nut, avocado, coconut, sweet almond and jojoba. You can also squeeze a wheatgerm capsule into the mixture for additional vitamin E.

Mineral oils, such as baby oil, are not generally suitable for massage as they just tend to lie on the surface of the skin. Carrier oils also provide lubrication so that when you are massaging the skin, your hands slip over it easily and lightly.

OILS OF LEMON AND EUCALYPTUS

Probably the second most popular way of using essential oils is in the bath. A few drops of pine, neroli or jasmine oil in a tub of hot water can be energizing, relaxing, sensuous — depending on the oil you choose. Add a total of no more than five drops of your oil, or mixture of oils, to the water just before you get in. Stir the water and then lie back and enjoy the experience for a minimum of 15 minutes.

Another, extremely therapeutic way of using essential oils is as room vaporizers, when

Rosemary

the scent is gently dispersed and you are barely aware of breathing it in. Commercial burners are available. These consist of a small container that should be filled with water and up to five drops of essential oil added. This is then placed above a candle or nightlight. When the flame burns, the oil is warmed and vaporized, dispersing through the room. You can achieve a similar effect by sprinkling a few drops directly on to a light bulb or adding them to a saucer of water placed on top of a radiator. You can also buy a fitment that surrounds a standard lightbulb and is designed to take a small quantity of essential oil.

Other ways of scenting a room and enjoying the effects of essential oils include filling a pump-action spray — the sort used on the leaves of houseplants — with water and three or four drops of oil and misting the air.

Lavender oil comes from the flowers, leaves and stems of the plant and helps to alleviate insomnia.

Rosemary

Chamomile

Direct inhalation is another popular method of using essential oils. At critical times, you can simply unscrew the top of the bottle and sniff. When suffering from a bad cold or cough, for example, fill a bowl with hot water, add a few drops of the appropriate oil, cover your head with a towel, close your eyes and inhale deeply for several minutes. This also works very well as a beauty treatment. The steam rising from the hot water opens the pores of the skin and you can use an essential oil for a facial in this way. Two or three drops of eucalyptus oil on the pillow at night should ensure a snuffle-free rest and a couple of drops of lavender can help immeasurably in counteracting insomnia. You can also sprinkle your handkerchief or a tissue with a couple of drops of calming, energizing or decongestant oil to sniff during the day.

Cold compresses are an age-old remedy for relieving the pain of bruising, muscular stress, headache and rashes and for reducing inflammation and fever. Pour 600 ml of cold water into a bowl and add six ice cubes. Add five drops of the appropriate oil, wring out a clean cloth or flannel and place it over the sore area.

A hot poultice works in much the same way for relieving muscular pain, ear ache, back ache, tummy ache, sore throat or congestion due to colds and 'flu. Fill a bowl with 600 ml of very hot water and add five drops of the appropriate oil. Wear rubber gloves for wringing out the flannel or cloth and make sure it is not scalding hot when you apply it to the skin. When the cloth has cooled to blood temperature, wring it out in the hot water and apply again.

Essential oils can be used in a wide range of beauty treatments. Facials have already been mentioned and you can also use essential oils in cleansers, masks and moisturizers to reduce oiliness and rejuvenate the skin. Some essential oils are excellent for treating dull and lifeless hair, dandruff and other scalp conditions and thinning hair. A little lemon oil can be added to water for a manicure and you can create a sensuous footbath by adding a few drops of essential oil.

Essential oils are excellent to use around the house and many of the natural antiseptics make good cleansers. You can add a drop or two of essential oil to rubbish bins to keep

Essential oils are excellent to use around the house and many of the natural antiseptics make good cleansers.

OILS OF LEMON AND GERANIUM

them clean and sweet-smelling. Make an easy pot pourri with dried flowers, grasses, seed-heads and few drops of essential oil. A couple of drops of oil on a cotton wool ball can be placed inside the vacuum cleaner bag to scent the air when you are cleaning the floors and stairs. Use the deodorizing properties of essential oils by placing a cotton wool ball with a few drops of oil inside your wardrobe and laundry basket.

There is almost no end to the ways in which essential oils can be used – from insect repellent to making your own personal perfume.

Massage

I F YOU bang your knee, almost automatically you rub the sore place. Touch is an instinctive human response to comfort and soothe, yet in modern society we tend to try to avoid coming into body contact with other people. Massage is a wonderful way to restore the balance.

An aromatherapy massage combines the effects and advantages of the two senses – touch and smell – more than doubling the benefits of both.

The best way to learn how to massage is to attend a basic course of classes taught by a qualified masseur. However, if you use your common sense and follow a few basic rules, you can give a more than merely adequate massage. First, find a comfortable, warm place. Massaging directly after a hot bath, when mus-

An aromatherapy massage combines the effects and advantages of the two senses – touch and smell.

cles are already loosened and the skin is readier to absorb the oil, is ideal. If you are massaging someone else, he or she needs to lie on a firm but comfortable surface at a height that will not strain your back. Cover any parts of the body that you are not working on with a blanket.

Essential oils must be diluted with a carrier oil and never applied neat to the skin. Add a maximum of 10 drops of essential oil in total to 20 ml of carrier oil in a dark glass bottle. Shake well to mix and keep the top closed when it is not in use. Carrier oils also lubricate the skin and help your hands glide gently. Do not mix up too much massage oil at any one time and store it in the refrigerator.

Warm the oil before use by immersing the

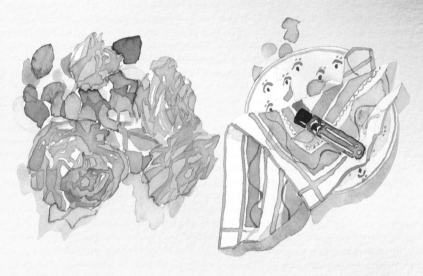

OILS OF ATTAR OF ROSE

bottle in a bowl of hot water. Alternatively, pour a little into the palm of one hand and rub your hands together to spread the oil.

The secret of a good massage is rhythm. Keep your hands moving all the time, either as mirror images of each other, one clockwise and the other anticlockwise, for example, or with one following the other, as if a single continuous movement. Do not rush. It does not matter if you keep repeating the same strokes.

Never do anything that is painful and try to avoid tickling. Do not massage directly over the bones of the spine and change the stroke if the person you are massaging does not like what you are doing. It is better to avoid hard, pommelling strokes and chopping with the sides of the hands. These can be beneficial but are better left to a trained masseur.

A basic back massage

OUR BACKS have to be one of the most abused parts of our bodies. Virtually everyone benefits from a back massage and, as this is the single largest area of the body, it is an easy one to approach. It is not possible to massage your own back – this is one area where you need your partner or a close friend.

The person being massaged should lie face down on a firm surface with his or her head turned to one side (do not use a pillow). Cover the lower half of the body with a blanket. Oil your hands.

First make long, light sweeping movements up the back with the palms of your hands, using your fingertips gently to feel where muscles are knotted and there are areas of tension. Move in sweeping half circles, up to the shoulders, down the sides and back to the waist in a calm rhythmic manner.

Next, diagonally slide your hands across the back from hip to torso on each side of the spine. You can press a little harder as you do this, but under no circumstances cause discomfort.

Work up each side of the body, gently pulling the skin from 'under' to 'over' using your left and right hands alternately. Tuck your fingers underneath as far as they will easily and comfortably fit, without digging in your nails, before pulling up and across. Then work across each shoulder in turn, from upper arm to neck, with the same flowing movement. Let one hand follow the other in a single continuous rhythm.

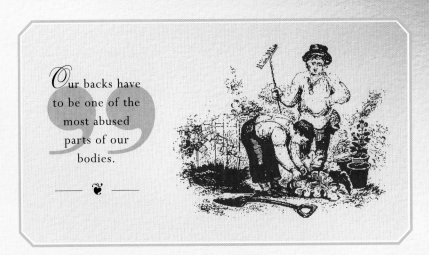

Our backs have to be one of the most abused parts of our bodies.

Using just the pads of your thumbs, make small circular motions from the top of the back to the waist, with one hand each side of the spine. One thumb works clockwise, the other anti-clockwise. Do not massage directly over the vertebrae.

Ask the person being massaged to bend back his or her arm, and rest the back of the hand on the middle of the back. If it is comfortable, rest his or her elbow on your knee. Make small, gentle, circular movements with the pads of your thumbs underneath the sticking-out shoulder blade.

Repeat with the other arm and shoulder. Using the index finger and thumb of each hand, lightly pluck the skin all over the back. Do not pinch or pull hard. Then gently knead the flesh from the buttocks across the lower back and up to the shoulders with your knuckles. Follow with a series of light presses using the 'heels' of your hands.

Place your index and third finger either side of the spine and repeatedly run your hands, one after the other, down the back from neck to buttocks. Finally, brush over the entire back in very light, feathery movements.

A basic foot massage

NO OTHER organ in the body is subject to such hard wear as our feet. If you make your feet feel good, the rest of your body will feel wonderful, too. You can give yourself a foot massage without any difficulty or you can massage someone else's feet. Work through the entire massage routine on one foot before starting on the other.

Make sure you are warm and comfortably positioned so that you do not have to stretch your back unreasonably to reach. Rest one foot, sole upwards, on the opposite knee if you are massaging your own feet. A hot, scented footbath first will make poor neglected feet feel pampered and soften the skin so that it absorbs the oil more easily.

Oil your hands and rub the heel vigorously between the palms. Do not press hard. Then lightly stroke your foot between the palms of your hands, from toes to ankle, with one hand above and the other below.

Using the pads of your thumbs, gently knead the delicate skin under the arch. Then make gentle, sweeping strokes from the ball of the foot to the heel.

Grasp the ball of the foot with one hand and the heel with the other and gently wring your foot as if squeezing out delicate laundry.

Move your foot from your knee and support it with your hands, one underneath the back of the heel and the other holding the toes. Gently flex it upwards and downwards several times. Then move it from side to side without forcing it.

A hot, scented footbath first will make poor neglected feet feel pampered.

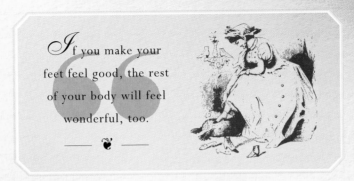

If you make your feet feel good, the rest of your body will feel wonderful, too.

Return your foot to its original position resting on the opposite knee. Support the side with the palm of one hand and gently pull each toe with the finger and thumb of the other hand. Keep the movement gentle. Then inter-link the fingers of your hand with your toes and work them backwards and forwards. Finally, press your toes hard against the palm of your hand.

Now place your foot flat on the floor or on a stool. Wrap your fingers under the sole and place your thumbs on the top. Gently rotate your thumbs over the entire top surface of your foot. Push your thumbs in opposite direc-tions up and down the entire length of your foot to pull the skin in opposite directions.

Return your foot to its position on your knee. Make a fist of the opposite hand and press it into the sole with a firm kneading movement. Work from the ball of the foot, down to the arch and back again.

Encircle the ankle with your fingers, press and hold for a count of four before releasing. Repeat several times. Using the fingers of both hands, wring your ankle like delicate laundry. Then with the tips of two fingers, make light, feathery circles, starting from the inner ankle bone, moving slowly around the back of the heel and ending at the outside ankle bone.

Finally, place one hand above and the other below the foot and stroke it repeatedly between the palms from heel to toes.

A word of warning

ESSENTIAL oils are a sheer delight and can be highly therapeutic. However, they are very potent. Never apply them undiluted to skin and do not exceed the stated number of drops.

If an oil causes irritation, wash the skin immediately and apply a little almond or other bland oil to the affected part. Symptoms should disappear within an hour. People with known allergies should consult a qualified aromatherapist before using essential oils.

Essential oils can be used effectively on children but dosages should be reduced as specified opposite. Use only lavender and chamomile oil for babies. Tea tree oil may safely be added to the list for children over one year old.

For babies under one year, use only one drop of the appropriate oil for a compress, in a warm bath or in a room vaporizer. You can also add one drop to 15 ml of carrier oil for massaging.

Use between one and three drops of oil in the same way for children aged one to six years. Use half the number of drops recommended for adults for children aged between seven and twelve. Children over twelve may use essential oils as directed for adults, but introduce new ones slowly and keep an eye open for any reactions.

Babies and children love the tactile closeness of massage and it can often help when they are tired, or fractious from minor illnesses. When massaging babies and children, use only your fingertips. Never apply any pressure, particularly to the vulnerable abdominal area and soft bones. Make sure the body is kept warm.

There are some conditions when massage

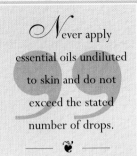

*N*ever apply essential oils undiluted to skin and do not exceed the stated number of drops.

is not recommended. Do not massage anyone – child or adult – with an infection or fever. Avoid massage following surgery or in the cases of a broken bone or an open wound. Do not massage anyone with skin eruptions, such as eczema, acne, nettle rash or heat rash. A bath with essential oils may, however, prove helpful; consult a qualified aromatherapist first. Do not massage anyone with a history of acute or chronic back pain. Some essential oils need to be used with especial care. Cinnamon, clove, hyssop and sage oils should be used only by a qualified aromatherapist. Do not use basil, clove, cinnamon, fennel, hyssop, juniper, marjoram, myrrh, peppermint, rosemary, sage or white thyme oils during pregnancy. However, very gentle massage with suitable safe oils during both pregnancy and labour can be very helpful in relieving discomfort and pain. Use only half the normal recommended quantity.

See the oil-by-oil guide for more details.

*C*innamon, clove, hyssop and sage oils should be used only by a qualified aromatherapist.

Geranium

Pelargonium graveclens and *Pelargonium odorantissium*

SOMETIMES known as rose geranium, the oil is extracted from the flowers and leaves of a shrub native to Madagascar.

It has a sweet, floral scent and is an attractive pale green colour. It is a mildly antiseptic oil that is useful for treating many skin conditions, either by adding a few drops to the bath, as a steam facial or a massage. It is an exceptionally good oil for women and has proved helpful in alleviating period pains and the misery of PMT.

Emotionally, it is a balancing oil that works both as a tonic and as a calming influence. Massage with geranium oil is an excellent way of treating sudden changes of mood. Massaging the neck and shoulders or the face is also good for mature and dry skin.

It may safely be used at home. Geranium oil mixes well with most other essential oils.

FOR A RELAXING MASSAGE

2 drops geranium oil, 2 drops rose oil and 2 drops lavender oil in 20 ml carrier oil

USE FOR A FACE AND SCALP MASSAGE THAT YOU CAN DO YOURSELF OR AN UPPER BACK AND SHOULDER MASSAGE, IF SOMEONE ELSE WILL DO IT FOR YOU, TO RELIEVE ANXIETY AND RELAX AN OVERTAXED BRAIN.

Jasmine

Jasminum officinale

FOR A SENSUOUS BATH

3 drops jasmine oil,
3 drops sandalwood oil and
3 drops ylang ylang oil
THIS GLORIOUSLY SELF-INDULGENT BATH MIXTURE HAS INTIMATE, FEMININE OVERTONES, AS WELL AS BEING IDEAL FOR RELIEVING STRESS.

FOR A STEAM FACIAL

3 drops jasmine oil and 2 drops
ylang ylang oil in a bowl
of hot water
THIS IS A GOOD PRE-BEDTIME BEAUTY TREATMENT, AS IT WILL RELAX THE MIND WHILE TREATING THE SKIN.

SOMETIMES called the king of oils, this is extracted from the flowers of the plant. As these have to be hand-picked and it takes about 8,000 blooms to make a single gram of oil, it is understandably very expensive.

Used in a warm bath or for a gentle massage, jasmine oil is very therapeutic for all kinds of cramps and, diluted to half its usual strength, can be helpful during labour. Its uplifting and relaxing aroma is effective in treating PMT. Many negative feelings can be overcome by massage, baths or inhalation using jasmine oil. It is a delicious oil to add to a wood fire. Used in the bedroom, it is said to have aphrodisiac properties.

Jasmine oil is safe for home use. It mixes well with cedarwood, geranium, lemon, patchouli, rose, and sandalwood.

Lavender

Lavendula augustifolia and *Lavendula officinalis*

FOR A STEAM FACIAL

3 drops lavender oil, 3 drops geranium oil and 2 drops lemon oil in hot water
THIS IS AN EXCELLENT COMBINATION FOR TREATING OILY SKIN AND IS REFRESHINGLY ASTRINGENT WITHOUT BEING HARSH.

THE OIL comes from the flowers, leaves and stems and is cultivated worldwide. It is probably the best known of all the essential oils.

It is a good antiseptic and excellent for treating infections, insect bites and burns. Headaches, even migraine, respond well to lavender oil and inhaling a few drops on a tissue is a remedy for nausea.

Used in a hot bath, lavender oil helps alleviate stress and insomnia. Used in a cool or lukewarm bath, it is refreshing and enlivening. Massaging with lavender oil promotes relaxation.

Lavender oil is quite safe for home use. It mixes well with cedarwood, eucalyptus, geranium, jasmine, violet and ylang ylang oils.

FOR A SOOTHING FOOT MASSAGE

4 drops lavender oil and 3 drops rosemary oil in 20 ml carrier oil
RELAXES TIRED AND ACHING FEET AND REFRESHES FATIGUED SPIRITS AT THE SAME TIME.

Neroli

Citrus bigaradia

THE OIL is derived from the blossoms of the bitter orange tree and is named after the Princess of Neroli.

The essential oil has a fragrance that is a combination of bitter and flowery.

A natural tranquillizer, neroli oil is excellent for treating both long-term tension and short-term stress. It is deliciously relaxing used for just about any massage. It is also beneficial to the skin. A scented bath with a mixture of oils is wonderfully calming.

The sensuous smell of neroli makes it a perfect oil for scenting rooms. If you know that you are about to face a stressful situation, a couple of drops of neroli oil on a tissue, which you can inhale from time to time, can help you through a difficult period.

Neroli is a safe oil for home use and may be used during pregnancy. Store in a sealed, dark glass bottle in a cool place. Neroli oil mixes well with cedarwood, frankincense, geranium, lemon, patchouli, rose, sandalwood and ylang ylang oils.

FOR A

TRANQUILLIZING BATH

2 drops neroli oil, 2 drops rose oil, 2 drops lavender oil and 2 drops ylang ylang oil

THE COMBINATION OF THESE SUPERBLY FLOWERY FRAGRANCES AND WARM WATER IS IDEAL JUST BEFORE BEDTIME AFTER A TRYING DAY.

FOR

A RELAXING

FULL-BODY MASSAGE

3 drops neroli oil and 2 drops jasmine oil in 20 ml carrier oil

ALL STROKES SHOULD BE LONG, SMOOTH, RHYTHMIC AND SOOTHING WITH NUMEROUS REPETITIONS.

FOR A STEAM FACIAL

FOR MATURE SKIN

2 drops neroli oil and 3 drops rose oil in a bowl of hot water

WHILE YOUR SKIN BENEFITS FROM THESE PURIFYING OILS, ALLOW YOUR MIND TO UNWIND.

Rose

Rosa centifolia and *Rosa damascenea*

THE essential oil is extracted from the petals and is one of the most expensive.

It has a strong yet delicate, sweet smell. It is excellent for treating all kinds of depression. It is also effective against headaches and insomnia. It is excellent for the skin, particularly mature skin.

A neck and face massage is both a superb beauty treatment and a wonderful lift to the spirits. This double benefit is particularly valuable for sufferers of PMT and during periods of bereavement, when crying makes the face puffy. A full body massage is deliciously relaxing and gives sometimes neglected areas of skin a special treat. A few drops of rose oil in a warm bath helps treat headaches, allergies and hangovers.

Rose oil is excellent for scenting rooms, works well in an essential oil burner and is a good choice for a home-made flower-based pot pourri.

Rose oil is safe for home use. It mixes well with frankincense, geranium, jasmine, lemon, neroli, patchouli, sandalwood and ylang ylang oils.

FOR A FACE MASSAGE

2 drops rose oil, 1 drop violet oil and 1 drop geranium oil in 20 ml carrier oil

THIS IS AN EXCELLENT COMBINATION FOR TREATING WRINKLED OR PUFFY SKIN. USE YOUR FINGERTIPS ONLY.

Violet

Viola odorata

THE OIL is derived from the flowers and leaves. It has a delicate, floral smell and a few drops in a warm bath will clear the head and aid concentration.

A facial massage with diluted violet oil is both pleasurable and beneficial. It is good for treating open pores, blackheads, spots, thread veins, rashes and sore or irritated skin. It is so gentle that it can be used regularly night and morning to revive and rejuvenate the face and neck. It may be used for a gentle steam facial, too. Steam inhalation is also good for relieving headaches.

Violet oil is safe for home use. It mixes well with geranium, lime, rose and ylang ylang oils.

FOR A FACE AND NECK MASSAGE

3 drops violet oil and 2 drops rose oil in 20 ml carrier oil
SQUEEZE THE CONTENTS OF 1 VITAMIN E CAPSULE INTO THE MIXTURE FOR EXTRA RICHNESS.

FOR A STEAM FACIAL

3 drops violet oil and 2 drops lavender oil in a bowl of hot water
THIS IS A DEEP CLEANSING FACIAL THAT IS GENTLE ON EVEN THE DRIEST AND MOST DELICATE SKIN.

FOR A RELAXING BATH

4 drops violet oil, 2 drops rose oil and 2 drops ylang ylang oil
THIS IS A GOOD COMBINATION FOR EASING TENSION AND WORRIES AND RESTORING CONCENTRATION.

Ylang ylang

Cananga odorata

THE OIL is extracted from the flowers of a tropical tree. The name means 'flower of flowers'.

The essential oil has a strong, sweet floral aroma that is very sensuous. It is hypnotic and relaxing and is, therefore, used for relieving all kinds of emotional turmoil. It is also sometimes a useful skin and hair treatment.

An aromatic full body or back massage calms tension and counteracts negativity. A few drops of essential oil in the bath can reduce stress and alleviate fears.

Used in an essential oil burner, ylang ylang creates a sensuous, even romantic mood ideal for the bedroom. It is a deliciously aromatic room freshener in other parts of the house too.

Ylang ylang oil is safe for home use. It mixes well with frankincense, geranium, jasmine, lemon, neroli, patchouli, petitgrain, rose and sandalwood oils.

FOR A CALMING MASSAGE

4 drops ylang ylang oil, 3 drops jasmine oil and 2 drops geranium oil in 20 ml carrier oil

USE FOR A SENSUOUS FULL BODY RUB OR HYPNOTICALLY SOOTHING BACK MASSAGE.

FOR A RELAXING BATH

4 drops ylang ylang oil and 4 drops petitgrain oil

THIS RELIEVES TENSION AFTER A HARD DAY IN THE MOST LUXURIOUS WAY. IT IS ESPECIALLY APPEALING TO THE FEMALE NOSE.

FOR A BODY MOISTURIZER

2 drops ylang ylang oil, 2 drops jasmine oil and 2 drops sandalwood oil in 20 ml carrier oil

THIS IS ESPECIALLY EFFECTIVE FOR DRY SKIN ON ELBOWS AND KNEES.

Ginger

Zingiber officinalis

THE OIL is extracted from the root of a plant growing in the Caribbean, Africa, India and Japan.

It has a warm, spicy smell. It is warming, stimulating and also antiseptic.

It is an ideal oil to use for massage or in the bath in cold weather as it boosts the circulation. A foot massage is an excellent way of restoring tired feet. Hot poultices may be used to treat stiff muscles or a cold. Inhaling the oil on a tissue can relieve nasal congestion and it can be helpful when feeling nauseous.

Ginger is safe to use at home but it should always be used in moderation as it is very potent. Some skins show a sensitive reaction. It mixes well with bay, eucalyptus, jasmine, neroli, patchouli and rose oils.

FOR TREATING MUSCULAR PAIN

3 drops ginger oil and 3 drops eucalyptus oil in 600 ml hot water

SQUEEZE OUT A FLANNEL AND APPLY THE HOT POULTICE TO THE AFFECTED AREA. THIS IS ALSO EFFECTIVE FOR EASING A SORE THROAT.

FOR SCENTING A WINTER FIRE

4 drops ginger oil, 4 drops sandalwood oil and 4 drops orange oil sprinkled on 3 or 4 logs of wood

SPRINKLE THE OILS ON THE LOGS 15 MINUTES BEFORE LIGHTING THE FIRE FOR A DELICIOUS AROMA REDOLENT OF CHRISTMAS.

FOR A THERAPEUTIC BATH

2 drops ginger oil, 3 drops eucalyptus oil and 4 drops rosemary oil

HOT WATER AND WARMING OILS COMBINE TO EASE MUSCULAR ACHES AND PAINS.

Juniper

Juniperus communis

THE OIL is extracted from the berries of the juniper tree. Juniper oil is especially effective in treating women's problems. However, it should never be used during pregnancy. A few drops in a hot bath can help relieve the distress of PMT and menstrual cramps.

Massage with juniper oil is excellent for muscular pains and rheumatism, while a brisk rub is helpful for treating cellulite.

Juniper oil is also effective for toning oily skin.

Juniper oil is safe for home use for massage, baths, inhalation, hot poultices and cold compresses. Make sure that you buy essential oil of juniper, as there is a cheaper, less effective juniper oil available that is made from the needles and twigs of the tree rather than extracted from the berries.

Juniper oil mixes well with cedarwood, eucalyptus, frankincense, geranium, neroli and petitgrain oils.

FOR A STIMULATING BATH

3 drops juniper oil and 3 drops patchouli oil

THIS IS ESPECIALLY TONING IN A COOL OR TEPID BATH AFTER THE WEAR AND TEAR OF A HOT SUMMER'S DAY.

FOR TREATING MENSTRUAL CRAMPS

3 drops juniper oil and 2 drops clary sage oil in 600 ml hot water

WRING OUT A CLOTH AND PLACE OVER THE AFFECTED AREA. RENEW AS SOON AS IT HAS COOLED TO BLOOD HEAT.

Myrrh

Commiphora myrrha

THE OIL is derived from the resin of a tree native to the Middle East.

The essential oil has a rich and spicy smell, and is exceptionally good for treating skin problems. It is also helpful in relieving stress.

A few drops of myrrh oil in a warm bath provide a wonderful morale-boost. It is a good expectorant, so a hot bath or steam inhalation are effective ways of treating a chesty cough, or a few drops on a tissue may be inhaled.

Properly diluted with a carrier oil, it is excellent for massaging dry or mature skin. A facial massage can help combat wrinkles and other signs of ageing.

Myrrh oil is safe for home use but it should never be used during pregnancy. It mixes well with frankincense, neroli, patchouli, rose and sandalwood oils.

FOR MASSAGING MATURE SKIN

2 drops myrrh oil, 2 drops lavender oil and 2 drops neroli oil in 20 ml carrier oil

WHEATGERM OIL IS THE IDEAL CARRIER OIL. USE ONLY YOUR FINGERTIPS TO STROKE THE DELICATE SKIN AROUND THE EYES AND SIDES OF THE MOUTH.

FOR A RICH MOISTURIZER

3 drops myrrh oil and 2 drops rose oil in 20 ml carrier oil

THIS MAKES A GOOD MOISTURIZER FOR DRY SKIN. MIX WITH PEANUT OR ALMOND OIL FOR ADDED PROTECTION.

Tea tree

Melaleuca alternifolia

THE OIL is extracted from the leaves of an Australian shrub. The essential oil has a medicinal smell and is a non-irritating antiseptic. It is particularly effective in treating fungal infections and may also be used for burns and insect stings. Between one and three drops may be added to a warm bath to ease the discomfort of nappy rash in older babies and toddlers. Do not use it on babies under 12 months.

Because of its strong smell, it is not an ideal oil for massage, but is excellent for adding to baths or applying with a cold compress. Use it in a vaporizer when there is family sickness. It is also good for inhaling.

Tea tree oil is quite safe for use at home. It mixes well with eucalyptus, geranium, lemon and sandalwood oils.

Bay

Pimenta racemosa

WEST Indian bay oil is extracted from the leaves and berries of a South American tree. The oil has a strong, woody scent. It is mildly antiseptic and quite strongly astringent.

This is a particularly potent oil that may irritate the nose and throat, so it should be used in moderation and very well diluted. It is good as a decongestant when inhaled with steam. It is a useful oil, mixed with others, for massaging away muscular tension and for stimulating poor circulation. A gentle friction rub is an effective treatment for greasy hair or a flaking scalp. Bay oil is safe for home use in moderation and well diluted, although some people have a skin sensitivity to it. It mixes well with cedarwood, eucalyptus, lemon and sandalwood oils.

FOR A STIMULATING FOOTBATH

2 drops bay oil and 2 drops ginger oil

ADD THE OILS TO A LARGE BOWL OF HOT WATER, MIX AND THEN SOAK TIRED TOES AND ACHING ARCHES FOR 10 MINUTES TO PUT A SPRING IN YOUR STEP.

FOR A CELLULITE RUB

2 drops bay oil, 2 drops lemon oil and 4 drops lavender oil in 20 ml sesame oil.

MASSAGE IN LONG, FIRM STROKES UP THE THIGHS FROM THE KNEES AND OVER THE BUTTOCKS AND ANY OTHER PROBLEM AREAS. USE THE PALMS OF YOUR HANDS, ONE FOLLOWING DIRECTLY AFTER THE OTHER.

FOR A STIMULATING, MASCULINE BATH

2 drops bay oil, 2 drops cedarwood oil and 2 drops lemon oil

USE IN THE BATH OR MIX WITH A CARRIER OIL AND APPLY TO THE SKIN BEFORE SHOWERING.

Cedarwood

Juniperus virginiana

THE OIL is extracted from the wood of the tree and was used extensively in the ancient world.

Cedarwood oil has a pleasant, refreshing, woody smell and is a popular fragrance with men. Its astringent properties make it an effective oil for skin conditions. It is an excellent decongestant, which is especially useful in treating catarrh.

Cedarwood oil acts as a stimulating tonic on the spirits, whether used in the bath or for massage. Also it has a composing effect that helps with stress and poor concentration.

Some people find its scent exhilarating and very sensuous. It has a reputation as an aphrodisiac.

Cedarwood oil is safe for home use but it should be avoided during pregnancy. It mixes well with eucalyptus, frankincense, geranium, jasmine and lemon oils.

Chamomile

Matricaria recutita or *M. chamomilla* and *Anthemis nobilis*

THERE are many different varieties of chamomile. Chamomile is one of the gentlest and most soothing of all the essential oils. It is naturally anti-inflammatory and can safely be used to treat skin rashes and other problems. Its sedative effects can benefit those suffering from headaches and menstrual or menopausal problems.

A warm bath containing chamomile oil is a marvellous antidote to the stresses and strains of modern life. A massage at bedtime helps to counteract sleeplessness as does inhaling chamomile oil in hot steam. It is an excellent oil to use for a steam facial or to mix in with unscented moisturizer to treat sore skin. A cold chamomile compress is an excellent remedy for a headache.

Chamomile is a very safe oil for home use and is so gentle it can be used on babies and children, if properly diluted. It is especially valuable in relieving the irritation of infections such as chicken pox. Chamomile oil mixes well with cedarwood, eucalyptus, frankincense, geranium, jasmine and sandalwood oils.

FOR MASSAGING ACHING FEET

2 drops chamomile oil and
2 drops eucalyptus oil in
20 ml carrier oil

SOOTHE YOUR ABUSED FEET WITH SWEEPING STROKES AND GENTLE CIRCULAR PRESSES TO MAKE YOUR WHOLE BODY FEEL RELAXED.

FOR A STEAM FACIAL FOR A DRY SKIN

2 drops chamomile oil and
3 drops jasmine oil in a bowl
of hot water

THIS GENTLE AND SENSUOUS-SMELLING COMBINATION IS A REAL MOISTURIZING TREATMENT FOR DRY SKIN.

Clary sage

Salvia sclarea

ALTHOUGH a member of the sage family, clary sage should not be confused with sage (*Salvia officinalis*), which produces an essential oil that is not recommended for home use.

The oil is derived from the tips of the leaves and has a delicious nutty smell.

Clary sage oil is excellent for treating exhaustion and may be applied as massage oil or in the bath. Its scent has a euphoric effect, so it is good for tackling phobias, depression and listlessness. A massage with clary sage oil can be helpful for both counteracting feelings of negativity and arousing the emotions.

A warm bath with a few drops of clary sage oil can relieve PMT and is also effective for other aches. A face and scalp massage is helpful for tension headaches. It is good for skin conditions.

Properly diluted, clary sage oil is safe for home use. Do not use during pregnancy. It mixes well with patchouli, rose, sandalwood and ylang ylang oils.

FOR A COMPRESS TO REDUCE INFLAMMATION

3 drops clary sage oil and 2 drops geranium oil in 600 ml iced water

As THE SOOTHING OILS GO TO WORK ON THE BODY, THEIR COMPLEMENTARY SCENTS RELAX, SOOTHE AND UPLIFT THE MIND.

Cypress

Cupressus semperverens

THE OIL is distilled from the leaves and cones of this Mediterranean tree.

Cypress oil is most helpful with menstrual and menopausal problems and can be used to treat both fluid retention and cellulite. It is a vaso-constrictor and may be good for dealing with varicose and broken veins.

Cypress oil is excellent for massaging the abdominal area and relieving discomfort. A bath with a few drops of cypress oil relieves the discomfort of piles. Menstrual problems are best dealt with by means of a hot poultice or an aromatic bath.

The smell of cypress oil is generally regarded as too overpowering to use as room freshener, but a few drops of oil on the pillow at night will ease breathing and stop coughing, and can be helpful in preventing bedwetting.

Cypress oil is safe for home use. It mixes well with bay, cedarwood, frankincense, geranium, lemon and sandalwood.

FOR A HOT POULTICE

5 drops cypress oil in 600 ml hot water

WRING OUT A FLANNEL AND PLACE ON THE ABDOMEN TO RELIEVE TUMMY ACHE OR MENSTRUAL CRAMPS. RENEW WHEN IT COOLS TO BLOOD HEAT.

FOR A PAIN-RELIEVING BATH

3 drops cypress oil, 2 drops geranium oil and 2 drops lavender oil

THIS COMBINATION CAN RELIEVE THE DISCOMFORT OF MENSTRUAL PROBLEMS OR CHESTINESS.

FOR A LEG MASSAGE

2 drops cypress oil, 2 drops lime oil and 1 drop lemon oil in 20 ml carrier oil

USE SWEEPING BUT GENTLE STROKES UP THE LEGS FROM ANKLE TO KNEE. USE ONLY THE FINGERTIPS ON SENSITIVE OR PAINFUL AREAS IF YOU SUFFER FROM VARICOSE VEINS.

Eucalyptus

Eucalyptus globulus

FOR A MASSAGE

FOR BACKACHE

*2 drops eucalyptus oil, 2 drops
lavender oil and 1 drop lemon oil
in 20 ml carrier oil*

FEEL OUT THE AREAS OF

TENSION WITH YOUR FINGERTIPS

AND RETURN TO THEM AGAIN

AND AGAIN.

THE OIL is extracted from the twigs and leaves of the Australian gum tree.

Eucalyptus has a distinctive aroma that instantly clears the head. Its decongestant effect has been employed in countless cold and cough remedies. It is a powerful antiseptic and is a warming oil for soothing muscular pains.

Steam inhalation or a few drops of the oil on the pillow at night can relieve cold and 'flu symptoms and help bronchitis. Heating eucalyptus oil in a vaporizer at night will help to make breathing easier and will disinfect the air. Eucalyptus oil can also be applied as a chest rub, provided it is properly diluted with a carrier oil, or as a hot poultice.

Eucalyptus helps heal sprains. It may be massaged directly on to the affected area, provided that it is properly diluted with a carrier oil first. A hot bath with a few drops of oil may also be helpful.

Eucalyptus oil may safely be used at home, but it is not recommended for people receiving homeopathic treatment. It is best used on its own, but can be mixed with bay, cedarwood, frankincense, geranium, lemon and sandalwood oils.

Frankincense

Boswellia carteri or *Boswellia thurifera*

THE OIL is extracted from the gum of a North African tree. Frankincense oil is especially useful in dealing with many of the symptoms of distress and panic. It helps restore a normal breathing rate and calms general nervousness. It is an excellent oil to use if you are feeling grumpy and is warming and comforting.

A face, neck and scalp massage provides effective relief for tension headaches. Steam inhalation is helpful for restoring good humour. A warm bath with a few drops of frankincense oil counteracts the effects of nightmares and sudden fears. It is often described as a rejuvenating oil.

Frankincense is safe for home use. It mixes well with cedarwood, eucalyptus, geranium, lime, neroli and patchouli oils.

Galbanum

Feurla galbaniflua

THE OIL is derived from a resinous gum. It is cultivated in the Mediterranean and North Africa.

The essential oil has a warm, woody smell. It is relaxing and soothing and makes a good stress reliever. It has a tonic effect and is useful in combating fatigue. Grazed and blemished skin responds well to it.

Mixed with other oils, such as frankincense or violet, it is excellent for a therapeutic face and neck massage. Mixed with chamomile or neroli, it is good for a shoulder or back massage to relieve nervous tension. It may also be added to a warm bath, mixed with other oils, such as lavender. Inhaling a few drops on a tissue is an effective tonic.

Galbanum oil is safe for home use. It mixes well with frankincense, geranium, neroli, rose and violet oils.

FOR A SOOTHING BATH

2 drops galbanum oil, 2 drops geranium oil and 2 drops lavender oil

THIS COMBINATION OF RELAXING, CALMING AND BALANCING OILS IS EXCELLENT FOR RELIEVING ANXIETY OR FRUSTRATION.

FOR A STEAM FACIAL

3 drops galbanum oil and 2 drops frankincense in a bowl of hot water

THIS IS A DEEP-CLEANSING TREATMENT ESPECIALLY SUITABLE FOR MATURE SKINS.

FOR A FACE AND NECK MASSAGE

2 drops galbanum oil and 3 drops neroli oil in 20 ml carrier oil

USE WHEATGERM OIL TO MAKE THE MIXTURE RICHER FOR MATURE OR BLEMISHED SKIN.

Patchouli

Pogostemon patchouli or *Pogostemon cablin*

THE OIL is extracted from the leaves and shoots of an Indian herb similar to lavender.

The fragrance is sweet, earthy and very persistent.

Patchouli oil is antiseptic and anti-inflammatory, so it is good for treating cracked skin, burns and scalp problems. Steam facials, hot poultices, cold compresses and aromatic baths are all effective.

Used in very small quantities, patchouli oil tends to be stimulating. In larger amounts, relatively speaking, it is relaxing. The oil is particularly useful, therefore, for treating tension and apprehension.

Patchouli is a good oil for scenting a wood fire. It is very pungent and heady.

Patchouli oil is safe for home use. It mixes well with frankincense, rose, sandalwood and ylang ylang oils.

FOR A MOISTURIZER IN WINTER WEATHER

2 drops patchouli oil, 2 drops sandalwood oil and 2 drops myrrh oil in 20 ml carrier oil

PROTECT YOUR SKIN AGAINST RAIN AND WIND WITH THIS MOISTURIZER. USE ALMOND OIL FOR SENSITIVE SKIN AND SUNFLOWER OIL FOR OILY SKIN.

FOR A SENSUAL BODY MASSAGE

2 drops patchouli oil, 3 drops geranium oil and 3 drops rose oil

DRAW THE CURTAINS, WARM THE BEDROOM, LIGHT THE CANDLES ... AND ENJOY.

Peppermint

Mentha piperata

THE OIL is derived from the leaves and flowers of the herb. The essential oil is refreshing and cooling, so it is excellent for treating all kinds of aches and pains, sore skin, insect bites and menopausal hot flushes. Its strong menthol smell is stimulating and it is helpful for overcoming fatigue, headaches, PMT and nausea.

Irritated skin can be soothed by soaking in a bath with peppermint oil. Use only one or two drops, as the oil is very potent. Equally, a cold compress may be applied to the affected area. It is a natural and effective painkiller, so baths, hot poultices and cold compresses are also helpful in treating various aches and pains. It is an ideal oil for a footbath or foot massage.

One of the best ways to use peppermint oil is to put a few drops on a tissue to inhale when you are suffering from a cold, a headache or any sort of nausea. Peppermint is also an excellent oil to use for purifying around the home. It works well as a room freshener.

Peppermint oil is safe for home use. It is particularly potent and should always be well diluted and in moderation. It mixes well with cedarwood, eucalyptus, geranium, lemon, patchouli, rose and sandalwood oils.

FOR A STIMULATING BODY RUB

1 drop peppermint oil, 1 drop myrrh oil and 2 drops lavender oil in 20 ml carrier oil

THIS WARMING AND ENERGIZING MASSAGE IS ONE YOU CAN DO YOURSELF AND IS AN EXCELLENT START TO A WINTER'S DAY.

Pine

Pinus sylvestris

THE OIL is extracted from the needles of several different species of pine tree.

The essential oil is very antiseptic and is excellent for treating coughs and colds. The stimulating, balsamic aroma has a long tradition of use against respiratory infections and pine oil remains one of the best inhalants.

Massage the chest with diluted pine oil for treating bronchitis, colds and a blocked-up nose. Or add a few drops of the oil to a warm bath and allow the aromatic steam plenty of time to work. This also helps relieve the pain of arthritis, rheumatism and muscular tension, as does gentle massage.

Pine is a good oil for a hot poultice. It may be applied to the chest or to swollen joints and aching muscles. It is useful around the house because of its deodorizing and antiseptic properties.

Pine oil is safe for home use. It mixes well with cedarwood, eucalyptus, frankincense, lemon, patchouli and ylang ylang oils.

**FOR A PAIN
RELIEVING MASSAGE**

3 drops pine oil, 3 drops eucalyptus oil and 3 drops frankincense oil in 20 ml carrier oil

RUB VERY GENTLY INTO SORE JOINTS, BUT YOU CAN USE FIRMER, DEEPER STROKES FOR EASING ACHING MUSCLES.

FOR A RELAXING BATH

3 drops pine oil, 2 drops chamomile oil and 2 drops lemon oil

THE AROMA OF THIS COMBINATION APPEALS PARTICULARLY TO THE MALE NOSE.

Rosemary

Rosmarinus officinalis

THE OIL is extracted from the flower tops and leaves of the herb.

It has a fresh, woody scent that is stimulating for both body and mind. A bath with a few drops of rosemary oil is an excellent tonic for lethargy and poor concentration. Its strong, minty aroma is helpful in alleviating the symptoms of bronchitis, and other breathing problems.

Rosemary oil has very warming properties and a massage with it is a good way to treat muscular aches. Other 'cold' conditions that respond well to rosemary are chilblains and poor circulation.

Many shampoos incorporate rosemary oil in their ingredients. For home hair care, add two or three drops to the final rinse for glossy, healthy hair.

Rosemary oil is generally safe for home use, but make sure that it is properly diluted. Some skins are sensitive to it. Do not use during pregnancy or if suffering from epilepsy. It mixes well with bay, eucalyptus, lemon, lime, neroli and sandalwood oils.

**FOR A HOME
HAIR TREATMENT**

*2 drops rosemary oil, 1 drop
lavender oil and 1 drop bay oil in
20 ml almond or olive oil*
USE FOR A SCALP MASSAGE,
WORKING THE MIXTURE WELL
INTO THE ROOTS OF YOUR HAIR.
COVER AND LEAVE FOR 30
MINUTES BEFORE SHAMPOOING
AS NORMAL.

Sandalwood

Santalum album

THE OIL is derived from the roots and wood of the tree. The essential oil has a sweet woody smell and it has been a popular ingredient in perfumes for many centuries.

It is a deliciously sensuous oil and a full body massage is a treat. It helps relieve listlessness, insecurity, and tension, and also helps restore lost libido. An added bonus is that the oil is good for dry or chapped skin. A warm bath with a few drops of sandalwood oil is deeply relaxing, and helps insomnia.

The oil is good for treating coughs, colds and congestion. A hot bath or steam inhalation helps clear mucus and a hot poultice relieves the pain of a sore throat.

It is an excellent choice as a room freshener and is one of the best oils for scenting a wood fire.

Sandalwood oil is safe for home use. It mixes well with frankincense, geranium, jasmine, patchouli, petitgrain and rose oils.

FOR A BEDTIME MASSAGE

3 drops sandalwood oil and 2 drops chamomile oil in 20 ml carrier oil

A SOOTHING MASSAGE OF SHOULDERS, SCALP, FOREHEAD AND TEMPLES SHOULD ENSURE A NIGHT OF SWEET DREAMS.

FOR A STEAM FACIAL

3 drops sandalwood oil and 2 drops rose oil in a bowl of hot water

THIS IS A DEEP MOISTURIZING TREATMENT THAT IS PERFECT FOR NORMAL AND COMBINATION SKINS.

Bergamot

Citrus bergamia

T HE OIL is extracted from the rind of a small, orange-like fruit from Italy.

It has a light, uplifting scent and is good for treating anxiety, and negativity. It is mildly antiseptic and so helpful with most aspects of skin care. It is an effective deodorizer, which makes it an excellent choice for scenting a room. It is good for ridding clothes of persistent underarm odour; simply sprinkle a few drops along the seams. At times of stress, discreetly sniffing a few drops on a tissue will do wonders for your confidence. This is also effective against travel sickness.

Bergamot is safe for home use. However, the pigment in the skin reacts to sunlight after bergamot has been applied, so do not go out-doors for three hours after use. Always dilute well. Bergamot oil mixes well with bay, lemon, lime, neroli, sandalwood and ylang ylang oils.

Lemon

Citrus limonum

THE OIL is extracted from the rind of the fruit. It has a tangy, citrus scent that is refreshing and invigorating and is a good pick-me-up first thing in the morning or whenever you are feeling under the weather. It is antiseptic and strongly astringent and has a reputation for treating warts, corns and veruccas. A hot poultice prepared with a few drops of lemon oil performs wonders for tired and aching feet.

The fresh-smelling oil is excellent for banishing the 'cob-webs', and inhaling a few drops on a tissue clears the head. A hot citrusy bath on a cold winter night stimulates the circulation. Massage with lemon oil will leave you feeling energized and is also a good treatment for cellulite.

Its fresh, clean smell makes lemon oil ideal to use around the house.

Lemon oil is safe for home use. It is strongly astringent, so should be used in moderation. It causes the skin to react to sunlight, so it is best to avoid going outside for two or three hours after use. The oil has a tendency to oxidize, so store it in a dark bottle in a cool place. Lemon oil is very strong, so it does not mix well with many other essential oils.

FOR MASSAGING FEET WITH CORNS OR VERUCCAS

2 drops lemon oil and 3 drops tea tree oil in 20 ml carrier oil
THIS CAN BE EFFECTIVE IF USED OVER A PERIOD OF TIME, BUT WILL NOT WORK MAGIC OVERNIGHT.

FOR A STIMULATING SUMMER BATH

3 drops lemon oil, 3 drops rosemary oil and 3 drops peppermint oil
A COOL BATH IS A REAL PICK-ME-UP AFTER A TIRING SUMMER'S DAY.

Lemongrass

Cymbopogon citratus

THE OIL is extracted from a wild grass that is now widely cultivated for the perfume industry.

The essential oil has a warm, citrus smell that is less sharp than lemon oil.

It is an excellent choice for treating skin eruptions and can also heal areas of inflammation. It can be used for a stimulating aromatic shower. Mix with a carrier oil as for massage and rub into your skin before getting under the water. It is ideal for adding to baths as it will boost circulation and help control excessive perspiration. Its deodorizing properties also make it a useful room freshener.

Lemongrass oil is an effective insect repellent. Its advantage over citronella is that it does not smell so strongly. You can apply it diluted in a carrier oil to your skin or put a few drops on the hems of curtains. Placing a cotton wool ball with a few drops of lemongrass oil inside the rubbish bin has a double benefit: it deodorizes and keeps away flies and wasps.

Lemongrass is safe for home use. It mixes well with frankincense, geranium and jasmine oils.

FOR A STIMULATING MASSAGE

2 drops lemongrass oil, 3 drops orange oil and 1 drop rosemary oil in 20 ml carrier oil

THIS SUMMERY COMBINATION OF OILS IS IDEAL FOR AN INVIGORATING BACK OR SHOULDER MASSAGE.

FOR A THERAPEUTIC FOOTBATH

4 drops lemongrass oil and 4 drops lavender oil in a large bowl of hot water

USE THIS TO CONTROL EXCESSIVE PERSPIRATION OF THE FEET – OR HANDS.

Lime

Citrus aurantifolia

T HE OIL is extracted from the rind of the fruit before it ripens.

It has a sweet citrus smell that is not quite so sharp as lemon oil, and is especially appealing to men. It is a warming and stimulating oil with antiseptic properties.

A vigorous massage with lime oil is excellent for treating poor circulation and cellulite. A gentler massage can help relieve the discomfort of varicose veins. A few drops of the oil in a warm bath is also effective in helping these conditions and relieves the symptoms of colds and 'flu.

Properly diluted in a carrier oil, lime oil may be rubbed on the chest for colds, on aching joints to relieve rheumatism or as an astringent on greasy skin. Steam inhalation reduces breathing problems.

Lime oil is safe for home use but should be used in moderation. It may cause a skin reaction in sunlight, so it is better not to go outdoors for three hours after use. Store in a dark glass bottle in a cool place. Lime oil mixes well with cedarwood, frankincense, geranium, lemon and violet oils.

**FOR MASSAGING
VARICOSE VEINS**

*2 drops lime oil and 2 drops
cedarwood oil in
20 ml carrier oil*

YOU CAN RUB THE SOLES OF YOUR FEET QUITE VIGOROUSLY, BUT USE ONLY LIGHT PALM STROKES AND FINGERTIPS ON SENSITIVE ANKLES AND SHINS.

Orange

Citrus sinensis and *Citrus aurantium*

THE OIL is extracted from the rind of the fruit. The fruity-smelling essential oil is cheering and refreshing. It is an excellent oil for reviving the spirits and dealing with lack of energy. It has a rejuvenating effect on the skin.

An orange oil massage is an excellent pick-me-up at the end of a working day before a busy evening. It refreshes and calms, but without sending you to sleep. A warm bath with orange oil will have a similar effect. A time-saving refresher when you are rushing from one appointment to another is to relax with a cold orange oil compress, preferably lying down with the feet raised.

It is a delicious oil for scenting a wood fire, which is a subtle way of calming fractious children. (Orange oil should not be used in any other ways for children under the age of 12.)

A facial massage, moisturizing treatment or steam facial using orange oil will benefit a dull complexion and help smooth away wrinkles. It also makes an excellent body moisturizer, but should be used in moderation.

Orange oil is safe for home use but should be used in moderation, as it may irritate the skin and cause it to react to sunlight. Store in a sealed, dark glass bottle. It mixes well with cedarwood, lemon, myrrh, patchouli and sandalwood oils.

Petitgrain

Citrus aurantium amara

THE OIL is derived from the leaves and twigs of the bitter orange tree.

The essential oil has a sharp orange smell. Its tangy aroma is both relaxing and stimulating, so it is an excellent oil for counteracting sluggishness, fatigue, insomnia and tension.

A shoulder and neck or back massage with petitgrain oil is an effective remedy for muscular or nervous tension. To counteract fatigue and help cure insomnia, a bath with a few drops of the oil is both relaxing and pampering. Inhale a few drops from a tissue when energy is flagging. This is also an effective antidote to nervousness.

Petitgrain oil is safe for home use for massage, baths and inhalation. Store in a dark glass bottle in a cool place. It mixes well with eucalyptus, lemon, lime, sandalwood and ylang ylang oils.

FOR AN ANTI-TENSION MASSAGE

2 drops petitgrain oil, 2 drops lavender oil and 2 drops sandalwood oil in 20 ml carrier oil

USE SLOW, GENTLE MOVEMENTS ON THE NECK, SHOULDERS AND TEMPLES.

FOR A REVIVING FACE MASK

2 drops petitgrain oil, 2 drops lemon oil and 2 drops ylang ylang oil in 20 ml iced water

MIX WITH SUFFICIENT GROUND ALMONDS TO MAKE A SMOOTH PASTE AND APPLY AS A FACE MASK. ALLOW TO DRY AND THEN RINSE OFF.

FOR RELIEVING MUSCULAR PAINS

3 drops petitgrain oil and 2 drops eucalyptus oil in 600 ml hot water

WRING OUT A CLOTH AND APPLY AS A HOT POULTICE TO AREAS OF MUSCULAR TENSION OR CRAMPS. RENEW WHEN IT COOLS TO BLOOD HEAT.

At-a-glance guide

TOP OILS FOR MIXING

chamomile

geranium

jasmine

lavender

neroli

sandalwood

ylang ylang

TOP BATH OILS

chamomile

frankincense

geranium

lavender

lemon

neroli

peppermint

ylang ylang

TOP THERAPEUTIC OILS (BODY)

bergamot

chamomile

cypress

frankincense

lavender

myrrh

rose

tea tree

TOP THERAPEUTIC OILS (FACE)

chamomile

juniper

lemongrass

orange

TOP OILS FOR INHALATION

chamomile

eucalyptus

frankincense

lavender

myrrh

peppermint

TOP OILS FOR ROOM SCENTING

bergamot

eucalyptus

geranium

jasmine

lavender

neroli

peppermint

sandalwood

ylang ylang

TOP HOUSEHOLD OILS

cedarwood

eucalyptus

geranium

lavender

lime

peppermint

pine

TOP OILS FOR HOT POULTICES

bay

clary sage

cypress

eucalyptus

galbanum

ginger

juniper

lavender

lemon

lemongrass

lime

petitgrain

peppermint

pine

rosemary

tea tree

TOP OILS FOR COLD
COMPRESSES

bergamot

cedarwood

chamomile

clary sage

eucalyptus

geranium

lavender

neroli

patchouli

rose

tea tree

violet

TOP OILS FOR A
THERAPEUTIC
MASSAGE

chamomile

clary sage

eucalyptus

peppermint

rosemary

sandalwood

TOP OILS FOR A
RELAXING MASSAGE

eucalyptus

frankincense

orange

petitgrain

jasmine

lavender

neroli

rose

ylang ylang

TOP OILS FOR
AN INVIGORATING
MASSAGE

bergamot

lavender

lemon

orange

peppermint

petitgrain

TOP OILS
FOR DEPRESSION

bergamot

clary sage

frankincense

geranium

jasmine

lavender

myrrh

neroli

rose

sandalwood

ylang ylang

TOP OILS
FOR CHILDREN

chamomile

lavender

tea tree

OILS UNSUITABLE
FOR HOME USE

cinnamon

clove

hyssop

sage

OILS TO AVOID
DURING PREGNANCY

basil

clove

cinnamon

fennel

hyssop

juniper

marjoram

myrrh

peppermint

rosemary

sage

white thyme

OILS UNSUITABLE
FOR STEAM FACIALS

bay

clary sage

ginger

juniper

pine

tea tree